The Village Sunc

With brief sketches of three of its scholars

John C. Symons

(Editor: Daniel P. Kidder)

Alpha Editions

This edition published in 2024

ISBN : 9789362999856

Design and Setting By
Alpha Editions
www.alphaedis.com
Email - info@alphaedis.com

Contents

PREFACE.

The writer of the following pages makes no pretension to authorship. He is deeply conscious that many defects characterize his production; and he hopes that they will be treated with the consideration which so candid an avowal merits, and which the fact demands.

The narratives are substantially true; but, for obvious reasons, the names of persons and places are changed.

The reason why this little book is sent into the world is, the writer considers the details which it contains of an exceedingly encouraging character, and calculated to support and strengthen the pious teacher in the discharge of his important and sometimes discouraging duties.

The writer has felt the need of encouragement while laboring in the Sabbath-school; and he has had that need supplied in no small measure from the consideration of the facts now before his readers. He hopes that the effect which these facts have had upon his mind, will be produced upon the minds of all who may peruse these pages. If such be the case—if but one devoted, self-denying teacher derive encouragement—his end will be more than answered.

With earnest prayer that the great Head of the Church will grant his blessing upon this little work, the writer submits it to his reader.

CHAPTER I.

THE VILLAGE—THE NEW SUNDAY-SCHOOL—THE SUPERINTENDENT—A REVIVAL.

M—— is a small village in the west of England, delightfully situated in a wooded pleasant valley. Through it runs the parish road, which—as it leads to the seashore, from whence the farmers of that and the neighboring parishes bring great quantities of sand and seaweed as manure—frequently presents, in the summer, a bustling scene. The village is very scattered: on the right of the beautiful streamlet which flows silently down the valley, and runs across the road just in the centre of the village, stands an old mill; which for many a long year has been wont to throw out its murmuring sound, as the water falls over its broad and capacious wheel. On the other side of the stream, and just opposite the old mill, a few yards from the road, stands a neat, commodious, and well-built Methodist chapel, which, from the prominence of its situation, and good proportions, has often attracted the eye of the passing stranger.

It was about the period when my narrative commences that the chapel was built. For many years the Methodists had preached in the village, and there had been a small society under the care of an aged patriarch, whose gray hairs and tottering frame bespoke the near approach of the last enemy: soon he came, and suddenly removed that good man to "the palace of angels and God." In consequence of the preaching-place being far out of the way, and the place itself—an old barn—anything but inviting, there had been for many years but little success.

In 18——, two or three zealous brethren from another part of the circuit settled in the vicinity of M——, and steps were at once taken to get a favorable site, and to raise subscriptions towards building a chapel as speedily as possible. The neighboring "squire" was waited upon by two of the new members, with whom he was personally acquainted; when, without hesitation, he gave them the spot of ground on which the chapel now stands. The chapel was soon built, and opened for divine worship; and many of the old members, who had witnessed the introduction of Methodism into the village, were constrained to exclaim, "What hath God wrought!"

The village, though small, was surrounded by a populous neighborhood, and many of the friends were anxious for the establishment of a Sabbath-school. In this they had many difficulties to contend with; arising principally from the awful carelessness of parents about their children's spiritual welfare, and the want of adequate help to carry on a school. However, they determined to make an attempt: and, accordingly, at no great period after the new chapel was erected, a school was established. As the society was small, pious teachers could not be secured, and they were under the necessity of employing persons of good moral character, or of abandoning the school altogether.

Few, perhaps, are more sensible of the advantage of pious teachers, than myself: and, whenever it is possible, I would have no others in a school. How is it to be expected that a teacher, careless—at least comparatively so—about the salvation of his own soul, can faithfully and earnestly enforce the duty of salvation upon his young charge: and yet this is the principal design of Sabbath-schools. It is not so much to teach the children to read,—though this is a great object,—nor even to give them a superficial acquaintance with the Bible; but to lay before, and as it were rivet upon, their minds the practical duties of Christianity. How can one who loves not the Lord Jesus Christ, successfully enforce the duty of love to God with the whole heart, and soul, and mind, and strength? How can one who knows nothing of the saving faith of the gospel, successfully exhort his children to believe on the Lord Jesus Christ? For, as he does not feel the necessity of these and kindred truths himself, he cannot enforce them so as to win the affections, and touch the hearts of the children. But of the privilege of pious teachers, M——Sunday-school was deprived.

The superintendent was a man well known and much respected, and was eminently qualified for his arduous task. With the exception of the senior female teacher, he was the only decided person in the school. He had much to contend with: and I am sure, from my own observation, had many been situated as he was, the school would have been speedily abandoned. He resided about a mile and a half from the chapel, but morning and afternoon, winter and summer, wet or dry, he was at his post! The numbers which attended the school might have been about seventy. The teachers, considering that they were not members of society, were pretty attentive for a year or two; but after that they began to fall off, and frequently was the superintendent obliged, in addition to his regular duties, to place the senior boys of the first class over the lower ones, and take the remainder, with the second class, under his own care. Laboring under so many disadvantages, it cannot be expected that M—— Sunday-school should in any respect be very prosperous: yet this I may say, that though I have been connected with Sabbath-schools for some years, and have had an opportunity of examining several, I have rarely ever met with a more orderly set of children, or a better conducted school.

But who, from such a school as this, would have expected anything like success? and yet the sequel will show, that, even under such unfavorable circumstances as these, God did not fail to work for his honor and glory!

The senior class of boys consisted of about a dozen promising lads, whose ages varied from nine to fourteen. They were placed under the care of two respectable moral young men, but who, with very many excellent qualities, were devoid of religion. The boys were encouraged to commit to memory portions of Scripture, for which they received small rewards; and thus a spirit of emulation was created as to who should possess the greatest number of these. Among those who distinguished themselves were three brothers, named James, Thomas, and George. James, the eldest, remained but a short time in the school: but Thomas and George continued much longer, and learned the whole of the three first Gospels, and part of St. John. They were very regular in their attendance, and when in school behaved just as others did, only that for their generally correct answers in the catechetical exercises, which usually followed the reading of Scripture, they were almost constantly at the head of the class. They had comparatively little time during the week; but often on a Sabbath morning have they repeated one or two hundred verses of Scripture. And here let me remark, that Thomas has since assured me, it was not a love for the Scriptures, nor a desire to become acquainted with them, which induced him to commit such large portions, week after week, to memory! it was a desire,—a kind of emulation,—to be at the head of the class, and to be thought highly of by his teachers and the superintendent. In this he gained his reward; for he was looked upon by them as the most promising lad in the school.

There was one thing connected with M——Sunday-school, which is worthy of notice and of imitation. The superintendent never dismissed the children without giving them a short address of from five to ten minutes. It was usually his custom on these occasions to impress upon the mind of his young hearers some important truth, through the medium of an interesting anecdote, or some well-conceived figure; so that, though the remarks he made might be soon forgotten, yet the anecdote and subject illustrated by it remained, and will, I doubt not, be remembered to the latest period of their lives by many of those who were privileged to listen to him. I am thoroughly satisfied that an effectual method of reaching the ear and the understanding of children, is through some such medium as that used by the superintendent of M—— Sunday-school. I hope the period is not far distant, when it will be more generally adopted.

A few years ago, the village of M—— was visited with a very gracious revival, during which a great number were soundly converted, most of whom have continued steadfast in the faith. Many of the teachers and scholars were among the number of those who gave their hearts to God.

The following extracts show the extent and reality of the revival:—

"There has been," writes the superintendent, "an extensive revival in this circuit. On Friday, the Rev. Mr. V——preached at this place. A prayer-meeting was held after the sermon, when several began to cry aloud for mercy—one professed to have obtained pardon. We have held prayer-meetings nearly every night, and a very gracious influence has rested upon us. We had, on one occasion, no less than twelve penitents crying to God for the pardon of their sins, amongst whom are some of the most thoughtless in the neighborhood. So many of our teachers and scholars were under conviction, that we did not think it proper to have school in the morning, but held a prayer-meeting, at which the presence of God was eminently felt, and several cried aloud. Nearly every female teacher or scholar, in our Sunday-school, is convinced or converted, and some of the males also. Glory to God!"

On another occasion he writes,—"Our revival still continues, though we have not had any crying aloud for mercy lately, but every time we meet in class we have some new members. The numbers, small and great, who had begun to meet in class, amounted to nearly one-third of our general congregation—their ages vary from eight years old to above sixty. Mrs. R.'s, our sweet singer, was a delightful conversion. She had long been seeking the Lord sorrowing. One morning she went into a neighbor's house, to inform them that a young woman had found peace: while in the house she was herself constrained to cry for mercy. One of the leaders was called in to pray with her, and, after a severe struggle, she found peace. The next Sunday I asked her (for she was singing delightfully) whether it was not sweeter to sing as she did, than before? She laid her hand on her breast, and with uplifted eyes, said, 'Yes, it is indeed, for I have often been condemned while singing words in which my heart did not join, but now I can sing with all my heart.'"

One of the teachers, writing to a friend, says, "You will rejoice to hear that the work of God is steadily progressing in this part of his vineyard. Many are found crying, in bitterness of soul, 'What must I do to be saved;' while others are enabled to adopt the language of inspiration, and exclaim, 'O Lord, I WILL praise thee; for though thou wert angry with me, thine auger is turned away, and thou comfortest me.' You will have heard that many members of Mr. T.'s family have been truly converted. Sunday-school teaching is now a delightful employment; most of our children are feeling the power of religion; and many of them, perhaps one-third, meet in class. Four out of seven, whom I teach, are, I trust, adopted into the family of God, and two others evince a desire to 'flee from the wrath to come.' I think I may venture to say there is not a family in the vicinity of our chapel, but has some one or more praying persons belonging to it."

It is exceedingly gratifying to know that the great majority of those who were converted belong to the school, continue steadfast, and are now pious and useful members of the Methodist Church.

CHAPTER II.

THE HISTORY OF JAMES.

There is a something connected with early associations which is almost indescribable. Every one has felt it, but few, very few, have been able to excel in a description of it! Who has not felt, as he gazes upon the cottage,—the home of his childhood,—his youthful days flash with all the vividness of reality before his mind; and as he stands and muses on the bygone years, numbered with those before the flood, he is almost spell-bound to the spot! All his childish pastimes and youthful pleasures pass in review before his mental vision; while the little trials with which his cup was mixed, are not without their influence in mingling a melancholy with the pleasing reminiscences of the past. Much has been said on this principle of association, and truly much remains unsaid on the subject. Scarcely is there a green sod, or a purling brook, a shady forest-tree, or a smiling flower, an enchanting and fairy landscape, or a barren and desolate heath; scarcely an object in nature, or a work of art, which does not awaken some gratefully pleasing, yet painful recollections of the past!

It is to this principle I attribute much of the good which results from Sabbath-schools. Often has the pious teacher to return from his onerous duties in the school, and retiring to his closet, to mourn on account of the fruitlessness of his efforts; and Satan never fails, at such seasons, to fill his mind with discouraging thoughts, which weigh down his spirits, and lead him almost to decide on retiring from the work. To such, let the precept and promise of God's word,—"Cast thy bread upon the waters; for thou shalt find it after many days,"—be a source of never-failing encouragement. How frequently, in after life, has it been found, that the instruction of the Sabbath-school, though it may have lain dormant for a time, has not been annihilated; but, through some circumstance, or by some object, it has been resuscitated in the memory, and it germinates, blossoms, fructifies, and brings forth glorious fruit, which has cheered the hearts and upheld the hands of many thousands of the most self-denying and arduous laborers in God's vineyard.

James, the eldest of the three lads mentioned, was a youth of considerable promise. He had one of the most retentive memories I have ever met with. Having reached the age of seventeen, his parents placed him with a Methodist in a neighboring town, as an apprentice. For twelve months after his removal, he stood aloof from all connection with the Church and people of God; after which period, as he remarks in a letter to his brother, "at the request of the superintendent of C—— school, I became a teacher in that school, and for four years remained as such." James continued as a teacher in the school for about twelve-months previous to his becoming a member of society; at the expiration of which time, he was induced, by the persuasions and invitations of his fellow-teachers, to meet in class. From this period he became a steady and devoted follower of the Lamb, and was at all times anxious to do what lay in his power to further the cause of the Redeemer. From his first connection with Sabbath-schools, when about five years old, he had conceived a love for them; and as he grew up his love and attachment to them increased, and his delight now was to devote all his energies to their promotion. As he more than once remarked to me, he conceived he was greatly indebted to Sunday-schools for the benefits he had received from them, and he determined, so far as in him lay, to discharge the debt of gratitude he owed.

His qualifications as a teacher were of no mean order. To an earnest desire for the salvation of his young charge, he added a large store of Scriptural and general knowledge, all of which was brought to bear upon the edification of his class. He was firm and resolute with his children, and at the same time kind and affectionate; so that I may safely assert that there were few, if any, more efficient teachers in the school than James. And the secret of the matter was this;—his heart was in the work; he delighted in it, and many of his happiest hours were those spent on the form with his class. The responsibility which he justly conceived attached itself to the Sabbath-school teacher, was shown by his attention to any of his own class who were sick; and not a few interesting records has he given of Sunday-school children, who, dying in the Lord, have left a bright evidence behind them that they are gone to glory.

Who can count the number of those who, through the instrumentality of Sunday-schools, are now before the throne of God, joining with angels, and archangels, and the spirits of the just made perfect, in singing, "Blessing, and honor, and glory, and power, be unto Him that sitteth upon the throne, and unto the Lamb forever and ever." Truly, there is no individual who verifies the truth of the Psalmist's declaration,—"He that goeth forth and weepeth, bearing precious seed, shall doubtless come again with rejoicing, bringing his sheaves with him,"—more frequently than does the pious Sunday-school teacher. Methinks I see him enter the paradise of God, met and surrounded by those who sat in his class, who listened to his teaching, and who were directed by him to "the Lamb of God who taketh away the sins of the world." Joyful indeed will such meetings be. O may such bliss be ours!

After serving five years as an apprentice, James removed to London. There are many persons who imagine, that to settle in London is the very acme of happiness; how little do such persons know of the reality! It is true, that in the religious sphere there are many advantages possessed by the resident of the metropolis. He has the teaching and counsel of ministers eminent for their piety, usefulness, and talent; he is brought into connection with some of the holiest and best men of the day; and, if his time be not altogether absorbed in the world, he has constantly numerous means of grace within his reach, so that he can frequently and delightfully join the great congregation, mingling his voice with theirs, swelling the anthems of praise and the solemn accents of prayer, as they rise like incense to the skies. But there is, on the other hand, much more allurement and temptation; there is everything around to draw away the attention from heavenly objects. Those with whom you have to associate, and who constantly surround you, are men of the world; men whose whole *delight* is in *forgetfulness* of God!—men, in many instances, whose whole energies are directed to ridicule, blaspheme, and overthrow the pious and devoted Christian; so that, being thus surrounded, the temptations of our great enemy are powerful, and often more fatal.

Many a promising young man within the range of my own limited acquaintance, has, through coming to London, made "shipwreck of faith, and of a good conscience;" and to any into whose hands this little work may find its way, let me earnestly and faithfully say, "Flee the very appearance of evil;" parley not one moment with temptation; but when tempted, fly at once to the cross, lay hold there, nor let that hold be loosened, till the enemy is vanquished, and your soul filled with perfect peace. Be particular what companions you have; "a man is known by the company he keeps." And let me warn you to be careful how you comply with the invitations of ungodly associates, in attending places of amusement and scenes of gayety. The wise man says, "My son, if sinners entice thee, consent thou not." Many and specious are the arguments which will be adduced to gain your consent; but take the precaution to ask yourself, honestly, and as in the sight of God, Can I get any good there? May I not get harm? Can I ask God's blessings upon it? Should I like to die while there? If these questions can be answered satisfactorily, then give your consent; but beware, even under those circumstances, how you choose for your companions those who know not God!

It was at the end of March, 18—, that James left his native country. On his arrival in London, he was at once provided with employment at a large establishment. Here he had much to contend with, being surrounded by, and brought into immediate contact with, a great number of men, many of whom were not only devoid of religion themselves, but ridiculed and sneered at those who made the least profession of respect for the commandments of God. Being known as a "Methodist," and refusing to work on the Sabbath, when ordered to do so, or leave his situation, he came in for a considerable portion of their obloquy and contempt.

CHAPTER III.

HISTORY OF THOMAS.

Thomas, the second brother, remained much longer in the school. Possessing a retentive memory, he learned the whole of the three Gospels of Matthew, Mark, Luke, and part of John. After remaining as a scholar for about three years, during which time he was often employed in teaching the junior classes, he was formally admitted as a teacher, in the presence of the whole school, the secretary delivering an interesting and affecting address to him, on the duties and responsibilities of his position as the guide of youth; at the conclusion of which he presented him with a book, entitled "The Guilty Tongue," as a reward for his good conduct and proficiency. Thomas had not long been a teacher, before a vacancy occurred in the first class, to which he had formerly belonged as a scholar, and he was at once nominated to it.

After continuing as a scholar for three, and a teacher for about two years, he removed to a neighboring town, as an apprentice. Absent from the parental roof,—placed in the midst of temptation, and surrounded by many allurements,—Thomas soon became forgetful of his former instructions, and his Sabbath-school engagements: instead of connecting himself with the school, and being found on the form by the side of his class, he might be seen ranging over the fields, and wandering through lanes, in company with those whom he had chosen as his associates. One thing is worthy of remark, and it shows the force of habit, and the power of early associations: he was regular in his attendance at the Wesleyan Chapel twice a day. This happened, perhaps, not more from choice than from a partial restraint which he felt, from the knowledge, that if he neglected this duty, it would come to the ears of his parents, and not only grieve them, but bring down on him their displeasure.

Though thus, for a brief space, led away into the sins of youth, Thomas was far from falling into what would be called gross sins.

The superintendent of the H—— circuit at this time was the Rev. J.R., a man who, in the work of the Lord, was instant in season, and out of season; and who was made very useful, not only by his public ministrations, but in his numerous and constant private visits among his flock, and the members of his congregation.

Under a sermon by Mr. R., addressed specially to the young, the subject of our sketch was powerfully wrought upon by the Holy Spirit, and awakened to a right sense of his danger as a sinner. But he strove to banish these convictions, and soon again became careless and indifferent to the great concerns of his soul's salvation.

About this period Thomas's father, anxious that he should become decided for God, told him he would send Mr. R. to visit him. But so averse was Thomas from seeing him, that he declared should Mr. R. walk in at one door, he would walk out at the other. However, Mr. R. called; and Thomas did not, and could not, put his threat into execution. Mr. R. urged upon him the danger of a course of sin,—the necessity and advantages of seeking God in youth,—and begged him to join his class, which met at seven o'clock on Sabbath mornings. Thomas promised to go; but when the morning came he broke his promise, and remained at home. In the succeeding week Mr. R. again called. Thomas again promised; and on the following Sabbath met in class for the first time. In about a month after joining the society, he was enabled to exercise faith in Christ, and obtained a clear evidence of his acceptance with God: this took place on a Sabbath evening, in company with one of his religious friends; while they were pouring out their souls at the throne of grace, light from heaven beamed upon his soul,—he was enabled to believe.

Connected with Thomas's joining the people of God, there is an incident not unworthy of mention here. A short time previously he had, with his elder brother James, paid a visit to their father's house. During that visit, the subject of union with God's people was strongly urged upon both of them by their parents. They had each been the subjects of the Holy Spirit's striving for some time, and were fully awakened to their danger and duty. While walking through one of the shady lanes situated between their home and the chapel, and conversing on the subject of religion, and the necessity of devoting themselves to God, Thomas said, if James would join the society he would. No immediate result followed; but about a fortnight before Thomas's connection with the Church, James had joined the Wesleyans, and had written to his father informing him of Thomas's promise. It was in consequence of this, that Mr. R. was requested to call on him; the result of which, through the blessing of God, was, as the reader has seen, his becoming connected with the Church.

Thomas had joined himself to God's people but a short time, when he determined, by the advice and invitation of his friends, to become a Sabbath-school teacher. His experience and success in this sphere of labor will be best described in his own words: "Soon after my union with the Wesleyans, I became a teacher in the Sunday-school, which, at that time, was not very prosperous. Here, as teacher of one of the junior classes, I strove to do my duty to God and the children placed under my care. A few of our teachers determined to establish a school at I——, a small village about two miles distance from H——, in which the Wesleyans had preaching at a private house, and a class of five members, to whom I willingly gave my assistance. But where should we get a room? was the next question to be solved. After some difficulty on this point, we got the use of an old barn; but which, by the way, had no window in it, and was consequently so dark, that we were obliged to keep the door constantly open, and, it being winter season, we found it very cold. Yet even this was too good to last long, for we were soon told that we could not have the barn any longer, and we were, therefore, obliged to look out for another place. Our next remove was to a different part of the village, to a room over some stables, the floor of which, besides having sundry large holes in it, was so rotten that we were obliged to range the children around by the walls, fearing lest the floor should give way from their weight, if placed in the centre. Even in such a place as this, our school increased from twenty to forty.

"After remaining in this room for some months, I may say truly, in continual fear of our lives, we removed to a much more commodious place, offered us by a Mr. H———, the only person in the village who was in circumstances of ease. But his love after a time grew cold, and we were surprised on our arrival one Sunday, to find that, without giving us the slightest intimation of his intention to do so, he had turned out forms, boxes of books, and all our paraphernalia, and locked the door; alleging as a reason, to the persons who lived at the next house—members of our society—that he wanted the place for potatoes; but to do him justice, I must add, that the room did not see a potato for many months after. I have before stated that we had preaching at the village, in a private house; the persons in whose house the service was held, were, I should say, both past sixty. They were poor, but excellent people. At the same hour with our school, the class used to meet at their house; and as they had only two rooms, it met in the one in which preaching was held. But no sooner did these good old people hear of our being turned out of our place, than they at once—before our arrival—got the forms and books into their house, and seated and arranged the children; so that you may judge of our surprise, when, on finding ourselves shut out from the one place, we were so unexpectedly put into the other. These noble-minded Christians consented that the class should meet in their sleeping-room, and that we should have the use of the other for our school. We could not allow such generous and self-denying devotion for the cause of God to go unrewarded, and we therefore determined to pay them a small sum per annum for the use of the room.

"I have not done with our difficulties yet. The road leading to the village was anything but a good one; indeed, in the winter it was very bad: so that, though in summer we could get plenty of teachers, yet when winter came we could get none, and the whole concern of the school then fell upon three or four. In the midst of our discouragements, one of our superintendents left us. The other was taken ill, and was prevented from being with us for six months. I was nominated to the office of our friend who had left, and excepting when a substitute could be found—which was not very often—I had to take the place of our sick one also: add to this the fact that we had only two other teachers who regularly attended, and you will see that our difficulties were of no light character. Often have I been at our little school with only one teacher and myself; and, indeed, at length things were come to such a crisis, that I said on my return home one afternoon, 'I will go no more; I'll give it all up,' But my friends reasoned with, and showed me the impropriety of such a decision; they told me that as the school was now entirely dependent upon myself for support, I should be much to blame if I gave it up. I listened to their advice, and continued to discharge my duties as well as I was able."

"Beware of desperate steps; the darkest day,

Live till to-morrow, 't will have pass'd away."

So sang Cowper, and so it proved in the case of I—— school!

"I determined," writes the subject of our narrative, "not to abandon the school. I made its position a matter of earnest prayer; canvassed our people for teachers; and God raised us up friends, so that soon we had a supply of teachers, and things went on smoothly. And here I would remark, that during the lack of teachers the attendance of the children was most gratifying, considering that most of them had to come a distance of from one to two miles, through roads which a 'Londoner' would consider almost, if not quite, impassable.

"Our little school, from this time, began to attract some notice, and we had an examination or two, had sermons preached, and gave the children an annual treat. This mode of procedure we found absolutely necessary; so that, by coming out prominently, we might draw the attention of our friends, and so reach their pockets.

"Our school continuing to prosper, we began to talk about a chapel, and several subscriptions were promised toward it; but in consequence of the landowner's antipathy to Methodism, we could not obtain a spot of ground to build upon. The death of the landowner, some time after, obviated the difficulty; a suitable site was obtained, and a chapel built, in which, a few years after, I had the pleasure of addressing the children on one of their festive occasions. The scene had changed, the new chapel which had been erected was well attended, the school prosperous, and the blessing of God evidently rested upon the place."

In my former narrative I made a remark or two on the evils and dangers to which a young man is exposed in coming to the metropolis, and the dreadful

"Well do I remember the day on which I became decided. It was on a Sabbath evening: I had been hearing a very faithful and powerful sermon from the Rev. Mr. G——, on the responsibility of individual Christians, and the duty of all to be employed for God. I saw my duty, and felt that I was grieving the Spirit by the course I was pursuing. I determined that I would open my mind to a friend with whom I was spending the evening. I did so; and the counsel I received was, 'Parley with temptation no longer; but to-morrow go to Mr. G., and open your mind to him,' 'I cannot do that,' said I. 'Then write to your leader,' answered my friend. This was just the advice I wanted; and I determined, by the help of God, to act upon it.

"Monday evening, at the close of business, I retired to my room; and after earnest prayer, commenced a letter to my leader. It was nearly finished: but on reading it over I was not pleased with its composition, and tearing it in pieces, commenced another. The agony of my mind was now at its height: my head seemed ready to burst; my brain was bewildered, and I was in a state bordering on distraction! While I write I seem almost to pass through this agony again. I finished a second letter! What I said in it I no more know than a child: I feared to read it over, lest I should be displeased with and destroy it, as I did the former. I at once sealed it up, and thrust it out of sight. I then threw myself on the bed, where I lay for a considerable time, till the exquisite excitement of the struggle being over, I retired to rest, thankful to God for the victory I had gained. In the morning my first work was to send the letter to my leader: after which I had another struggle with the powers of darkness. 'You cannot retract now,' whispered the enemy. 'You have done it; and now where are your sermons to come from? You know you have only two in the world: suppose you should make a failure in your first attempt, what a fool you would look like! how you would get laughed at!' But the step was taken, and I rejoiced to feel that I had done my duty: a load which had long been too heavy for me was removed, and I felt altogether a new man.

"I fear I have been tiresome; but I will now soon conclude. I was proposed at the local preachers' meeting, accepted, preached several times before the brethren, with some degree of acceptance; and after remaining about four months in Y——, from the period referred to, my health being re-established, I again removed to the metropolis, where my name was regularly inserted on the plan. Having passed my examination in the usual way, I was received into full connection as a local preacher. I need not tell you that I am now fully occupied in this blessed work; that my happiest hours are those spent in it; that, were it the will of God, I am willing to live and die in the work."

Thomas is now a local preacher in one of the London circuits; and although by his occupation he is necessarily prevented from much study, being in business, as unfortunately most young men are, from early in the morning till late at night, he is, nevertheless, an acceptable, and, it is hoped, a useful preacher.

CHAPTER IV.

HISTORY OF GEORGE.

The third brother, George, remained in M—— school for some years after the elder brothers had left. As a scholar he was well-behaved and attentive; and after conducting himself with propriety for a considerable period, he was appointed a teacher. He had not long been thus engaged before, during a gracious revival of religion in the circuit, he became deeply impressed with the necessity of salvation, and determined to seek the forgiveness of his sins. He joined the Wesleyan society, and after a short period, professed to have obtained peace with God through Christ, and the remission of sins through faith in his blood.

Shortly after he had joined the Wesleyan society, he was sent for some months to a boarding-school in a neighboring town. At that period the Rev. J.B. was one of the resident Wesleyan ministers. Mr. B. had, a little time previous, preached a sermon to the young; and at the close of the service had invited those young people who were not connected with any church, and who were determined to begin to serve God, to meet him on the ensuing Thursday evening. Thirty came, whom he formed into a class, and continued to meet while he remained in the circuit. To this class George united himself; and the instructions and kindness of this devoted minister, exercised a beneficial influence on his character and conduct. By the grace of God he was enabled to persevere amidst the enticements of his youthful associates, and to keep a conscience void of offense towards God and man.

Soon after this, he was removed from the parental roof, and placed with a local preacher at B., as an apprentice. Here his religious experience deepened, and he enjoyed more of the favor and love of God; continuing instant in prayer, and adorning the doctrine of God his Saviour. His Sabbaths were indeed days of rest; but not the rest of the idle, for he engaged heartily in the duties of the Sabbath-school, and was a regular and punctual teacher. Some of his friends, who knew the state of his health, were rather opposed to his leisure moments being thus occupied, and considered that he ought to take exercise and recreation in the open air. Such were not his views. He shortly had to remove from business for a time, and to take one or two sea voyages, which happily restored him to his former health, and enabled him to return to his duties.

After exercising as a prayer-leader as well as a teacher for some time, he became impressed with the conviction that it was his duty and privilege to preach the gospel. He was encouraged to proceed, and his name placed on the local preachers' plan. He then ceased to attend the Sunday-school.

In a letter to a brother, George observes: "I can scarcely remember anything of serious impressions while at school; though, I doubt not, the instructions I there received had a salutary influence upon my mind. If I remember rightly, several of the elder children were converted during the revival at M.; and most of those who continued steadfast were, or had been, connected with the school, either as teachers or scholars."

George was not satisfied with his attainments in the divine life, but sought to possess higher enjoyments and more extensive usefulness,—"to deeper sink, and higher rise, and to perfection grow." He was soon enabled to testify that "the blood of Jesus Christ cleanseth from all sin;" and had much delightful evidence that to be more holy was to become more happy and useful. He labors devotedly and successfully as a local preacher, and is determined to live to the glory of God.

I will only add,—and I rejoice that I am able to do so,—that each of the brothers is now actively engaged in the work of God. James is the superintendent and manager of a Wesleyan Sunday-school; and in point of perseverance, and constancy in the prosecution of duty, he is quite a pattern. Thomas and George are very acceptable local preachers in the Wesleyan connection. May they ever be zealous in every good work, and have grace to continue faithful unto the end.

"He that goeth forth and weepeth, bearing precious seed, shall doubtless come again with rejoicing, bringing his sheaves with him." Psalm cxxvi, 6.

"Cast thy bread upon the waters; for thou shalt find it after many days." Eccles. xi, 1.

APPENDIX.

The following letter has been put into the writer's hands since the preceding pages were in the press, and will be read with deep interest, as containing an account of the death of one of the teachers of T——street school, from the pen of her brother, James's colleague:—

"My beloved sister entered into the joy of her Lord about half-past twelve this morning. I sat up in company with Mrs. B. and another friend—it was a delightful night, there was a calm and cloudless sky, and the full moon shone in at the window in spite of the blind and rush-light. I rose at last, and extinguished it, and drew up the blind; it was a beautiful and a solemn sight! I shall never forget it. Jessy found it hard work to breathe, and at times, I almost indulged a wish that she might be speedily released. But I did not dare to pray for life or death; 'Thy will be done,' was my motto, and all was well. Seeing her eyes often turned upward, I spoke, and pointed upward,

'Yonder's your house and portion fair;'

she hesitated a moment, and then added,—'M—y tr—easure—and—my HEART are there.'

"At another time, observing her in great pain for the want of breath, and at the same time moving her lips in silent prayer or praise, I said,—'As thy day, so shall thy strength be,' She replied with feeling, 'Yes.' At another time we understood her to say 'Jesus,' with something like energy in her voice; but whether in prayer or praise we could not decide, as the voice was thick, and rather indistinct, although loud, and many words could not be understood because of this.

"The last word I caught was 'Glory,' and a very appropriate one it was to bid adieu to this lower world, and enter that which is above. I attempted to move her head a little, in order to let her see the beautiful moon once more, as it shone on every part of her, except just the forehead and eye; when she said, 'Don't bring me back from heaven,' and when we could not understand her words, we were convinced by the tone of her voice that pleasure and joy reigned within. Her hands had been for some time down by her sides; but a few minutes before death she raised them gently up, and clasping them together, seemed by her motions to commend her soul to Jesus. O! I shall never forget that scene: there lay the dying saint before my face,—it was the solemn, still hour of midnight—the calm serene without beautifully harmonized with the scene within. The virgin was ready, with her lamp trimmed, and the cry came, 'Behold the bridegroom cometh; go ye forth to meet him,' The summons was obeyed, and the faithful servant entered into the joy of her Lord.

"As regards my own feelings, I was without agitation; and that sweet, sweet peace, which is the peculiar property of the people of God, kept my heart and mind: but when the spirit had fled I felt a little excitement, and could have disturbed the house by shouting her dying word, Glory!

"She selected a verse for the funeral sermon; it is the last in the seventh of Revelation: 'For the Lamb which is in the midst of the throne shall feed them, and shall lead them unto living fountains of waters; and God shall wipe away all tears from their eyes.'"

THE END.

Milton Keynes UK
Ingram Content Group UK Ltd.
UKHW041821151124
451262UK00005B/714